Ernie Coombs:
Mr. Dressup

Trudy Duivenvoorden Mitic

Fitzhenry & Whiteside

Contents

THE CANADIANS®
A Continuing Series

Ernie Coombs

Author: Trudy Duivenvoorden Mitic
Cover Illustration: John Mardon
Design: KerryDesigns

THE CANADIANS® *is a registered trademark of Fitzhenry & Whiteside Limited.*

Fitzhenry & Whiteside acknowledges with thanks the Canada Council for the Arts, the Government of Canada through its Book Publishing Industry Development Program, and the Ontario Arts Council for their support of our publishing program.

National Library of Canada Cataloguing in Publication
Duivenvoorden Mitic, Trudy, 1954-
Ernie Coombs, Mr. Dressup / Trude Duivenfoorden Mitic.
(The Canadians)
Includes index.
ISBN 1-55041-498-4
1. Coombs, Ernie—Juvenile literature. 2. Television
personalities—Canada—Biography—Juvenile literature. 3. Mr. Dressup (Television program)— Juvenile literature.
I. Title. II. Series: Canadians.
PN1992.4.C66D83 2005   j791.45'092   C2004-906964-0

Printed and bound in Canada.
ISBN 1-55041-498-4

© 2005 Fitzhenry & Whiteside Limited
195 Allstate Parkway, Markham, Ontario L3R 4T8

Prologue

It's not surprising that a boy like Ernie Coombs grew up to become Canada's beloved Mr. Dressup. In some ways he'd been groomed for the position from the beginning. He grew up in rural Maine, where the coastline and countryside remain unspoiled to this day. His childhood was spent in the care of a loving and good-natured family. With his parents and brother he explored the backwoods and the seashore, his curiosity nurtured by the family's passion for nature and the environment. Out of this safe and happy childhood came a lifelong devotion to the teaching, guiding and entertaining of an entire nation's children.

Ernest (far right) came from a close and loving family

Ernie Coombs would have called himself an ordinary man who went on to have an extraordinary career, a fate he more than once said was the result of exceptionally good fortune. But fame didn't come instantly and easily. For more than a decade he knew the taste of hard work, living hand to mouth and travelling from one low-paying, short-term job to the next. He trained as a commercial artist but reinvented himself several times over until his Mr. Dressup character emerged in the mid 1960s.

Ernie Coombs receives the Order of Canada in 1996 from Governor-General Romeo LeBlanc

As part of the Mr. Dressup production team he played a major role in improving standards for children's television programming. Over the years the show never strayed far from its original formula: Children would be treated with dignity and respect. They would be spoken to as individuals, thus eliminating the "Hello Boys and Girls" approach common at the time. There would be no interruptions for advertisements and no Casey dolls marketed, and therefore no attempt to turn children into future consumers. There would be no violence, no confrontation and no preaching. The show would be about using one's imagination, being curious and resourceful, getting along and celebrating everyday life.

The formula was simple, and it worked.

Ernie Coombs's contribution to children's television has been acknowledged several times, first in 1994 when he won the prestigious Earle Grey Award, presented by the Academy of Canadian Cinema and Television. In 1996 he was awarded a Gemini for best performance in a children's or youth program or series. Later that year he received the "Children's Award" from the Children's Broadcast Institute. He also received the Order of Canada.

Ernie Coombs never set out to become a celebrity, and unlike many famous people, never learned to talk comfortably about himself. But he loved his work, believed in it, and did it so well that being a celebrity simply became part of his destiny.

Chapter 1
The Early Years

When Ernest Arthur Coombs was born in Auburn, Maine, on November 26, 1927, his American parents could not have imagined that one day he would be one of the most beloved Canadians of all time. Instead, they saw "Baby Ernest" as the perfect addition to their close-knit family and the ideal playmate for his two-year-old brother, Kenneth. Ernest and Kenneth, they envisioned, would grow up robust and happy in their rural Maine setting, never far from the rugged Atlantic coastline.

Ernest at age 2 with his older brother Kenneth

The boys' parents had also been born and raised in Auburn. Irma Hazeldean Emerson, an only child, had graduated from Bates College in nearby Lewiston and taught school until her marriage in 1920. Passionate about literature, she kept a journal throughout her life and penned long, captivating letters to family and friends. She rarely spoke ill of anyone and lived the lifestyle of a committed conservationist long before environmentalism became a popular cause.

"I was influenced a lot by my mother," Ernie Coombs would say many decades later. "She was the kind of person who found something great and wonderful in everything."

His father, Kenneth Brown Coombs, had an identical twin, Keith. Kenneth was a good-natured man who loved hiking,

Ernest's mother,
Irma Coombs

Ernest's father,
Kenneth B. Coombs

fishing and exploring the Maine outdoors. He had a flair for drama and acted in locally produced plays and later, in his college's theatre productions. Both Kenneth and Irma came from families that, while far from wealthy, recognized the value of a good education. After receiving a degree in chemistry from Bowdoin College, Kenneth married Irma and together they set out for New Jersey where he went to work for a chemical company.

Within a year the constant exposure to chemicals damaged his health and forced him to leave the job. The couple returned to Auburn for his recovery, then moved to Missouri where Kenneth began teaching at a private school for boys.

Two years later the school closed, bringing them back to Auburn. This time Kenneth found work just across the river at Bates Mill, a textile factory that made heirloom bedspreads. As the mill's chemist, he formulated the dyes used to colour the fabrics. It was during this time in Auburn that their two sons were born.

When Ernest was not yet a year old, his father was offered another teaching position, this time in the town of Waterville, 100 kilometres to the north. The family relocated to a modest house on 23 Pleasant Street, directly across the road from Waterville Junior High School. Kenneth taught science at Waterville for the next fourteen years.

Life was idyllic for the young Coombs boys. Their parents were happily married and shared the parenting and household workload. They quarrelled so rarely that it would be years before Ernest and Kenneth realized that bickering was not just something children did.

Almost as soon as they could walk, the boys began accompanying their parents on frequent hikes into the woods or down by the seashore, learning about the plants and animals

they encountered along the way. In the vegetable garden they sauntered alongside their dad who taught them about planting and harvesting. As they grew older, they rode their bikes around the neighbourhood and savoured the attentions of both grandmothers, who lived nearby.

The Coombs' house at 23 Pleasant Street across from the school where Ernest's father taught

The grandmothers were happy to keep the boys supplied all year round with their favourite foods, which happened to be Christmas treats. Grandmother Coombs knew the aroma of her gingerbread cookies never failed to draw the boys to her back door and Grandmother Emerson could make a delicious mincemeat pie in no time at all.

Kenneth and Ernest in front of their grandmother's cottage

Summer vacations were spent at Grandmother Coombs's seaside cottage, about an hour's drive along the coast. Capable swimmers at an early age, the boys spent hours at a time navigating the family rowboat around the sheltered cove.

Sometimes a cousin would come visiting and often a boy from a neighbouring cottage might amble by looking for adventure. One afternoon when both the cousin and

Young Ernest in a quiet moment

neighbour were around, someone suggested a game of cops and robbers. Ernest and his cousin, the designated robbers, were soon captured and tied to a sturdy tree. Abandoned there, they sounded out the usual tortured howls of protest while the "cops" snickered with satisfaction just out of sight. But then the robbers' cries for help grew so loud and desperate that, now suddenly concerned, Kenneth and his friend came running back to see what was causing the commotion.

Hanging like a giant, silvery ornament above the captives' heads was a nest releasing a large squadron of angry hornets. Some circled the orb in hot, ineffective rage; others dove downward to the easy, unfortunate targets. Quick-thinking Kenneth ran to get a bucket of water and doused the captives. With the hornets momentarily befuddled, he rushed to untie the boys who then raced on their heels to the ocean.

It took a few days for the stings to heal and perhaps a bit longer for Ernest to forgive his brother and cousin for choosing such a poor and hazardous "jail."

Ernest wasn't a clumsy youngster but his curiosity and enthusiasm sometimes had him courting minor misfortune. During a lively family game of croquet he tripped over a wicket and broke his arm.

On one summer outing the boys ended up in a relative's barn where a pig was penned in the corner. Not content with the view from the pen's side rails, Ernest clambered on top of a nearby lidded barrel for a better look. As he stepped on the lid's edge, it suddenly inverted and sent him sliding into the barrel—which happened to be full of sour milk. While the scolding was kept to a minimum, Ernest could not escape the rigorous scrubbing required before being allowed back into the family car for the ride home.

Another vacation took the family to a remote lake. Upon arrival everyone jumped into the water, Ernest landing on what was perhaps the only piece of glass for kilometres around. Although the nearest town was a considerable distance away, the cut in his foot was serious enough to take him there for medical attention.

Ernest and the family dog Tag

During his quiet times Ernest was a dreamer, content to play out adventures and dramas in his imagination. Eventually he began crafting little movie sets and taking pictures of them. He also started lessons on the clarinet, an instrument the family dog, Tag, never learned to appreciate. A boisterous springer spaniel that lived up to its name, Tag joyfully accompanied the brothers almost everywhere. In winter they often skated at the local rink and skied the nearby hills and meadows. Skiing often meant avoiding collisions with Tag who had the disturbing habit of darting back and forth in front of anyone venturing down a hill on skis.

Ernest's childhood years were carefree and uncomplicated. Like many of his friends he didn't have much in the way of material goods, but he knew what it felt like to be cherished and respected. Nothing could have prepared him better for his future career.

Chapter 2

From Ernest to Coombsie

Ernest's flair for drawing and cartooning was already beginning to emerge by the time he was old enough to attend Waterville Junior High School. Although this talent won the admiration of his peers, his habit of doodling in class often irritated the teachers who felt that school was strictly for learning and paying attention. When one teacher also happened to be his father, Ernest discovered he would be treated the same as everyone else, with fairness but no tolerance for fooling around.

The same code of conduct applied at home. When Ernest came in one afternoon and announced he wasn't feeling well, his observant father detected a faint drift of tobacco odour in

Ernest with his parents and Grandmother Coombs

the air. "Have you been smoking?" he asked sternly. By way of reply Ernest began throwing up. He and a few young friends had spent the last hour sampling a cigar and he was now feeling desperately queasy. While the nausea might well have been punishment enough, he nonetheless had to endure a long, grim lecture on the evils of tobacco.

36 East Elm Street where Ernest and his family lived in Yarmouth, Maine

Ernest was generally a good-natured lad but he did have a quick temper that occasionally flared and got him into trouble. One winter evening when he was about thirteen years old, he came home to find everyone away and the doors locked. His own house key, which he had forgotten to take with him, was locked somewhere inside. Although he knew the others would be back soon, waiting in the cold was not an option that appealed to him. So instead he splintered the panel of the back door with a well-placed kick and let himself in. It was quite some time before he was allowed out with his friends again, and it took even longer for his weekly allowance to be reinstated.

Ernest cared little about fashion and often went to school looking somewhat less than trendy. His brother, on the other hand, had an eye for stylish clothes and took pride in his neat personal appearance. The contrast between the two was obvious enough that Kenneth became known as "Joe Flash" while

Ernest (front row, far left) played clarinet in the student orchestra

Ernest, to his own amusement, was given the nickname, "Joe Slopp."

In 1942, when Ernest was fifteen, the American government became actively involved in the Second World War. To help with the war effort, Ernest's father quit teaching and began working at the shipyards in Portland, a city near the Maine–New Hampshire border. The family moved to nearby Yarmouth and Ernest enrolled at North Yarmouth Academy, a high school with a student body of about twenty-five.

While his slight build, dark-rimmed glasses and disregard for fashion might have kept another student shyly on the sidelines, Ernest's wit and sociability soon had him fully involved in the school scene. Before long he'd earned the nickname "Coombsie" and made several friends with whom he would stay in touch for the rest of his life. He didn't participate in sports but played clarinet in the student orchestra and put his artistic skills to use drawing posters and designing table centrepieces for school dances.

Ernest also volunteered as art editor for the school's biweekly newspaper and as before, continued to doodle in class. Before the end of the year he announced to his friends that he would one day be a commercial artist.

There was no doubt Ernest was suited to such a profession, but he was also an endearing comic who kept his friends entertained with an easy, spontaneous wit. He had a very keen sense of what was funny and never resisted an opportunity to inject humour into everyday life. He loved innocent pranks and had a natural sense of timing when it came to telling jokes or making witty observations. His humour was easy and spontaneous, never mean and never directed at any individual person.

Not surprising then, when he got his first big laugh while addressing the students during a general assembly, he became hooked on performing. Before long he found himself immersed in the school theatre program. In the Gilbert and Sullivan operetta *The Pirates of Penzance* he flourished as the not-so-clever Sergeant of Police, one of only ten lead roles.

During another show, this time a slapstick comedy, Ernest walked down from the stage and into the audience toward one of his friends. He then pulled out a pair of scissors and cleanly snipped off the boy's tie just below the knot. The friend had

Ernest (front row, right) in 1944 with the North Yarmouth Academy News staff

*Ernest's 1945
graduation photo*

been warned to wear an old tie but, convinced Ernest would never actually go through with his routine, wore the best one he owned.

Socially Ernest was no more awkward with the girls than the other boys were. His circle of friends always included girls, who liked him for the same reasons his male friends did: a sharp sense of humour and an easygoing and unpretentious nature.

The graduation ceremony of 1945 saw Ernest sharing the school's top academic honours with his best friend, Charles Hatch. The time had come to say goodbye to North Yarmouth Academy. Already some of the local young men had begun receiving their draft notice, an official order to sign up for military service. The school days were over. The adult years were just beginning.

Chapter 3

Summer Theatre and a Taste of Television

D uring his years at North Yarmouth Academy, Ernest Coombs, like many of his friends, had signed up for volunteer duty with the Maine State Guard. Normally state-related defence functions were performed by the country's National Guard. But these were the war years, and with the National Guard called away to the country's defence, it was left to the state to provide its own security and contribute to the nation's protection as well. Maine responded by forming the State Guard, made up of retired military officers and volunteers not yet old enough to be drafted into national military service.

One of the State Guard's duties was to monitor the state's airspace and coastline for signs of enemy infiltration. Ernest was part of a team that was taught to study the skies for enemy activity. Once he could successfully identify various friendly and enemy aircraft, he began volunteering for two-hour shifts in one of Maine's string of "spotting" towers. His watch was at two o'clock in the morning but being a typical teen, he wasn't put off by the nighttime hours. And, like his friends, he was making a valued contribution to America's war effort, which gave him purpose and nudged him closer to adulthood.

Private First Class Ernest Coombs in uniform

After graduating from high school Ernest signed up for two years in the military service. He served them at Clark Air Force Base in the Philippines where he worked as a weatherman. His desire to be a commercial artist did not diminish

Ernest at the family cottage in Maine

while he was away, and when he was released from the military in 1947 he enrolled in a two-year program at the Vesper George School of Art in Boston. This was followed by one year of studies at the University of Kansas School of Fine Arts. By 1948 he had completed his formal education and was ready to begin his career.

During his college years Ernest had spent the summer months back in Maine at the family's new seaside cottage in Round Pond. Always industrious, he would dream up projects that employed both his hands and his imagination.

One summer he decided to build a shed with his brother who had just completed a degree in architecture. Instead of driving to the hardware store for materials, however, the young men borrowed their parents' boat and set out to salvage what they needed from the bay. In those days it was not uncommon for boaters and vacationers to throw their junk and discards into the sea, so the brothers were able to find almost everything required for the shed. Floating planks were plentiful; even the odd window drifting by was not unheard of. Nails were pulled from salvaged wood and painstakingly straightened so they could be used again. In the end the only materials bought from the store were the roofing shingles.

Amid the construction, a cousin who was publicity director for a nearby summer theatre came by, looking for Ernest. Their play needed one more male to fill a small, non-speaking role. Would Ernest please come and do it?

Always ready for a new adventure, Ernest followed his cousin to the Boothbay Playhouse and was soon carrying out the assigned role. The part was so minor that he found himself with a fair bit of idle time between shows. Since idleness was not something he thrived on, Ernest began helping with set design and construction.

His employers were quick to recognize the value of an actor who could do double duty; in fact, that was how their type of theatre, known as stock theatre, operated. Instead of bringing in established actors from elsewhere, they hired local or "stock" actors who could perform a variety of tasks. These actors did the shows but also worked on the props, sets and lighting. It wasn't unusual to be the star one week and build sets a week later.

Such an arrangement suited Ernest so well that he returned to the Boothbay Playhouse for the next three summers. His routine often had him in the basement designing sets and painting scenery. On cue he would dash upstairs and on stage to deliver a line or two, then run back down to the basement to resume his painting. He was agreeable to any task that needed doing on or off stage and, unlike many actors, never worried about getting a starring role. After all, he was a set designer by trade, not an actor.

Up until now, even though he had enjoyed performing in high school, Ernest had never seriously considered a career in entertainment. But at Boothbay he gradually began rethinking

*Boothbay Playhouse
In Maine*

Walt "Bud" Littlefield

his future. Acting had always come naturally to him and he knew how to make an audience laugh. Perhaps, he thought, by combining his skill as a performer with his talents as an artist, he could make himself twice as marketable in the limited and intensely competitive entertainment industry.

A defining opportunity came in 1952, at the end of his fourth summer in stock theatre. As he was packing up to leave, the owners of the Boothbay Playhouse hired him to work on a show they were developing for a television pilot. The filming would take one week, sometime during the winter, in the nearby town of Harrison. During the filming all staff would be housed in a summer hotel. Unfortunately winter was well underway when they arrived and it soon became apparent why the hotel was only for summer use. Trying in vain to stay warm in their unheated room, Ernest and his roommate, Walt "Bud" Littlefield, huddled in their beds at night with all their clothes on. The floor was so cold that their feet ached as they readied themselves in the morning. Ernest took it all in good stride, making wry comments about their predicament and sculpting one of his blankets into a pathway on the floor between his bed and the chair on which he kept his clothes.

As if all this wasn't challenging enough, no provisions had been made for bathing. Predictably, everyone's personal hygiene had seriously declined by the end of the week.

Ernest and Bud had just met that week but already they were becoming good friends. As the filming was coming to an end, they were given the task of driving the rented camera equipment back to New York City. The Boothbay owners wanted it returned by 9 a.m. the next morning to avoid being charged another day's rent. So the minute filming was completed, the gear was loaded into Bud's 1952 Chevy convertible and the two friends started the 600-kilometre drive south.

By then it was already late afternoon and the feeble sun was fading into the wintry darkness. A snowstorm had started to brew; Ernest and Bud realized they were in for an all-night drive. Storms are a way of life in Maine so postponing the trip was not considered an option, not even when the storm swelled into a raging blizzard.

Gingerly, the friends made their way to Portland, stopping at Ernest's parents' house in nearby Yarmouth just long enough to change their socks and grab a few provisions. Throughout the night they inched along, past the Maine border and into New Hampshire, then Massachusetts, Connecticut, and finally New York State. They fought fatigue and sleep by turning up the radio and rolling down the windows to expose their faces to the pelting snow and frigid night air.

Finally they rolled into New York City just as the morning rush was getting underway. Triumphantly they delivered the equipment to its destination on time. Then they set off in search of a hot bath and some sleep.

In due time the pilot was viewed—and rejected—by the American television broadcaster, CBS.

Chapter 4
More Struggles and More Adventures

Over the next half decade Ernest's search for employment took him to regional theatres in various parts of America. When the acting jobs grew scarce, he fell back on his training as a commercial artist. Because he was "an artist who could also read blueprints" and "an actor who could also do scenery," he had an advantage over his colleagues and was never without work for very long. No job was too small or too unimportant for him, and every job was approached as an adventure. Most times the paycheque was modest, as little as fifty dollars a week, but Ernest never worried too much about

Ernie Coombs loved cars. Here he poses beside a Triumph TR3.

money and was rarely discouraged. By his own account these were carefree, nomadic years.

At one point he found his way back to Boston, a town he knew well because of his two years there as a college student. There was no work for actors and artists but fortunately he had other skills to fall back on. He'd been a car buff all his life and was a skilled amateur mechanic. Soon he was working at a garage, pumping gas and fixing cars. While the job was definitely a detour from his career path, it would do until something better came along. And as always, the comic within him was never far from the surface.

One day his pal Bud Littlefield decided to drive the four hours from Maine to Boston to pay Ernest a visit. They arranged to meet a group of friends at a restaurant for lunch. Ernest was at the garage and would join them as soon as he finished his shift.

The friends were seated at a window booth with a clear view of the sidewalk. They had already started eating when someone looked up and spotted Ernest strolling toward them, wearing a frayed, camel-hair coat. Ernest was still not much influenced by styles and trends. He wore what he liked, and this particular coat was a favourite possession.

Instead of stepping into the restaurant as expected, Ernest walked up to the window where his friends sat and pressed his face against the glass. They were used to his antics so pretended not to notice and continued eating. With exaggerated sadness, Ernest's eyes followed their hands as they lifted food from their plates to their mouths.

The waitress came by and was mortified to see a "vagabond" interfering with her customers. She offered to have him "removed."

"He's not bothering us," they told her, so she shook her head and shifted her attention to another table. At that point Ernest slipped inside and joined his friends at the table. When the waitress came by again and saw the vagabond now sitting with her customers and eating from their plates, her jaw dropped in disbelief.

Ernest's collage of odd jobs in Boston also included a stint as a fire extinguisher salesman. He managed to get his friend Bud hired for this job as well and together they were sent to work in the company's booth at a Boston trade show.

BOOTHBAY PLAYHOUSE

Ernest (2nd from left) and his first wife Margo (far left) with members of the Boothbay Playhouse

Bud had just purchased his first pair of elevator shoes, a new and popular fashion for men at the time. They resembled regular loafers but added a few inches to the wearer's height. Ernest, who was wearing regular loafers very similar to Bud's new shoes, wanted to try them on. They fit well so he wore them into the next booth and started a friendly chat with the saleswoman. Then he came back to his own booth, slipped into his own shoes and went out again to resume his conversation with the young woman. He went back and forth, switching shoes, until she was totally mystified. First he'd appear a bit taller, then she'd be the taller one. She kept glancing at his shoes as he came and went and while they talked, but Ernest pretended not to notice. Like the restaurant waitress, she was never let in on the prank.

Though Ernest was always light-hearted about his circumstances, by the mid-1950s he had grown weary of roaming from one job to another. At one point he even worked as a technical illustrator for Boeing Wichita, a manufacturer of commercial aircraft in Wichita, Kansas. But he was tired of living hand to mouth. He had seen much of the country through the windshield of his 1932 Auburn, an old car he'd bought for $550.

He had been briefly married to a young actress named Margo with whom he had worked at the Boothbay Playhouse. After their 1952 wedding he and Margo drove to California so he could meet her mother, then ventured all the way back east to New York City where they tried to settle down.

But settling down is difficult for those who make their living as actors, and Ernest and Margo often lived apart as one or the other found work in various theatres throughout the northeastern United States. Ernest was happy to work wherever there was an interesting job, including the Boothbay Playhouse. Margo wanted to stay in New York in the hope that she might someday be discovered and become a star. In time they began to drift apart and in 1954, after two years of marriage, they separated amicably.

Ernest was by then 27 years old. Somewhere along the way he had shed the formal childhood name "Ernest" and the high school nickname "Coombsie" to become simply "Ernie." He longed for some permanence and stability in his life.

Ernie Coombs was ready to be a grown-up.

Chapter 5
Children's Televison Comes of Age

Marlene "Lynn" Hodgkiss

By the late 1950s Ernie Coombs, now almost 32 years old, had moved to Pittsburgh, Pennsylvania, and was performing with the Knickety Knockety Players, a children's theatre group. There he met the first of two people who would change the course of his life. Marlene Hodgkiss, a graduate of the Pittsburgh Playhouse School of Drama, was an actor also working with the same group of performers. She was introduced to Ernie as "Lynn," a stage name her friends had given her after deciding it better suited her character. She adopted the name Lynn and for the rest of her life was known by that name, both on and off stage.

A spirited and energetic woman just barely out of her teens, Lynn was determined not to be left disadvantaged by her less-than-perfect, fatherless childhood. Ernie admired her resilience and asked her out. Although he was almost ten years older than Lynn, they soon fell deeply in love.

As the young couple was beginning to plan their life together, WQED TV in Pittsburgh, America's first educational television station, approached Ernie with an exciting offer. They needed a puppeteer for their new children's production, *Dimple Depot*. Would he be interested in the job?

Within days of Ernie's transfer to television he met the second person who would affect his destiny, Fred Rogers. Fred was producing and starring in *The Children's Corner* for WQED TV. His show, *Mister Rogers' Neighborhood*, was still in the future, but already he was beginning to turn heads with his new approach to children's programming. He was one of the first children's entertainers to base his work on the science of childhood development. Specialists in this area had discovered that, just as there is a normal pattern for physical growth and development in children, there are also many stages of mental and emotional development. It was found that preschoolers, for example, learn best when the format is slow, simple and repetitive.

Ernie and Lynn on their wedding day

Based on that research, Fred spoke directly and calmly to his young viewers. He talked in ways that children understood and at a pace they could follow. He offered them a safe, peaceful place to "visit" and helped build their self-esteem by making them feel special and unique.

Even though Ernie and Fred worked on different programs, they quickly became good friends. Ernie shared Fred's vision for children's television programming and both realized the importance of speaking to their home audience as individuals. Fred told Ernie to pretend there was one little boy or girl sitting just behind the camera, and speak directly to that one child.

Ernie and Lynn on their honeymoon in 1961

Cathie and Lynn, Christmas 1963

Ernie Coombs hadn't worn formal clothing in a good many years but on Saturday, May 13, 1961, he donned a brand new suit for his wedding to Lynn Hodgkiss. An equally dapper Fred Rogers stood as his best man.

Over the next two years Ernie worked at WQED and continued working in stock theatre between seasons. Summer holidays were spent on the beaches in Maine. A daughter, Cathie, was born in 1962. Life was very nearly perfect.

But the tide of destiny changed again when Ernie returned from summer vacation that year to learn that WQED was cancelling *Dimple Depot* and the TV station no longer had work for him. With a wife and baby, two dogs and a brand new car, Ernie realized his sudden unemployment could not have come at a worse time.

In Canada in the meantime, the newly created Canadian Broadcasting Corporation started taking a closer look at television programs made specifically for children. Television was then still in its infancy. While programming in general was limited, this was even more true for young viewers. Much of what was available to Canadian children consisted of "cowboy" shows beamed in from the United States. And many of them had noisy, mindless plots based on the inaccurate stereotypes of the time.

The CBC hired Dr. F.B. Rainsberry, a childhood education specialist, to evaluate the programs and he concluded that Canadian children would be better served by television that offered some substance and relevance. So he set out in search of new programs that would speak to

On the set of Butternut Square

young viewers instead of just offering empty amusement.

In Madison, Wisconsin, he found *The Friendly Giant*, a simple but dignified program that offered quiet and thoughtful entertainment through story and song. He convinced its creator, writer and star, Bob Homme (pronounced "Hummy") to transplant the show to Canada. The CBC began airing it in 1958.

In Pittsburgh Rainsberry discovered Fred Rogers's show, *The Children's Corner*. He found Fred's views on children's programming agreeable with his own and invited him to come to Canada where he could be the star of a new CBC children's

An early publicity "still" of Ernie Coombs

show, *Mr. Rogers.* Fred accepted the offer in 1963 and, knowing he would need another puppeteer, asked his recently unemployed friend, Ernie Coombs, to come along.

Ernie, eager for work and always open to a new adventure, soon settled his young family in Toronto. He spent the next season happily employed as part of the *Mr. Rogers* team, then had a few anxious moments when Fred Rogers decided not to renew his CBC contract. Fred returned to Pittsburgh where he would go on to transform the fledgling *Mr. Rogers* into the perennially popular *Mr. Rogers' Neighborhood.* Ernie was once again left without a job.

However, the CBC now had a void in children's programming that it needed to fill quickly. Just before leaving, Fred Rogers suggested that a program be built around Ernie Coombs. This seemed like sound advice to the CBC since it was already familiar with Ernie's work. It developed the concept for *Butternut Square* almost overnight, possible in those days because extensive analysis and testing was not yet required for every new program. Ernie Coombs, it was decided, would put away his puppets and become one of the show's stars. And so *Butternut Square* was launched the following season, in 1964.

Soon Ernie was devising different costumes for each show and along the way his Mr. Dressup character was born. Mr. Dressup sang, did pantomime, drew pictures and worked his way through the show's story lines with a colourful cast of human and puppet characters. Among them were Casey, a sprightly four-year-old not always in a cooperative mood, and his loyal dog, Finnegan. Their creator and puppeteer, Judith Lawrence, would go on to develop Casey and Finnegan into Canadian legends all their own.

In some ways *Butternut Square* was the first Canadian television show to be developed specifically for preschool-aged children. Just as Fred Rogers had done, Ernie was careful to speak to his audience as individuals, in a way that took their own feelings and experiences into account. The show's characters did not always behave perfectly. The plots and dialogue often dealt with everyday, ordinary issues to which the children at home could readily relate. The gentle pace gave young viewers time to develop their own thoughts on topics such as sharing, compromise, patience and disappointment.

The show was so popular with children and parents that when the CBC cancelled it in 1967 because of budget restrictions, a great outcry arose from the public and also in the federal government's House of Commons in Ottawa. "We love Mr. Dressup and Casey and Finnegan," the children cried to their parents. The parents expressed their own outrage: Here, finally, was a television character, Mr. Dressup, who respected children and related to them on their level. Here was a program created specifically for preschoolers, and the CBC wanted to take it off the air!

Amid the protest, the government ordered the CBC to come up with an alternate plan. The CBC, recognizing a unique opportunity to ease budget troubles as well as please their viewers, announced that it would reformat *Butternut Square* into a less expensive show. From now on, it was decided, Casey and Finnegan would be the only puppet stars. There would be just one main set and one story line per half-hour program. There would only be one non-puppet star, Ernie Coombs's Mr. Dressup character.

Thus a new children's television show was born. Appropriately, it would be named *Mr. Dressup*.

Chapter 6

Canada Meets Mr. Dressup

Mr. Dressup

When the show started on February 13, 1967, Ernie Coombs began a new relationship with CBC Television that would span the next three decades. Joined by Casey and Finnegan, the kind and patient Mr. Dressup quickly found his way into the hearts of Canadian children with his low key, personalized approach. Every Monday to Friday he was there at 10:30 in the morning, a reliable, trusted friend, inviting the viewer to come over and play.

He encouraged children to use their imagination and made

easily copied crafts from household items such as toilet paper rolls and egg cartons. A shoe box became a boat or a pirate's chest. Almost anything could be transformed into a musical instrument. Mr. Dressup was legendary for his scissors and the satisfying crunch they made as he cut through poster board and construction paper.

While his approach might have seemed simple and accidental, it was, in fact, very planned; the producers knew that much of their audience lived in rural and remote parts of Canada, including the Far North, and wouldn't have access to specialized craft supplies. They realized it would be frustrating and pointless for children to see craft projects being made on television that they couldn't duplicate at home.

Costumes, many of them created by Ernie, became an important part of the show. Soon there were so many that Mr. Dressup found he needed something for costume storage and presentation. Ernie was pondering this one day while waiting for the light to change at a Toronto intersection. Suddenly the words *"Tickle Trunk"* popped into his mind. He liked the catchy alliteration and promptly set out to buy an old steamer trunk at a secondhand store. He painted it bright red with colourful flowers and brought it home to Mr. Dressup's "house."

Trunks filled with interesting things have always fascinated children and the Tickle Trunk proved instantly popular with Mr. Dressup fans. Even when he took it on a road show for university students years later, his now grown-up audience would call out, "What's in the Tickle Trunk?"

In 1969 a radically new American program for preschool children burst onto Canadian television screens. Borrowing from the fast-paced dynamics of television advertisements or "commercials," *Sesame Street* focused on learning counting, the alphabet and social skills. The hour-long program consisted of several story lines in many snappy segments that featured rhythm, repetition and a new breed of puppets known as "Muppets."

When CBC Television began broadcasting *Sesame Street* the following year, there were many who predicted it would spell the end for *Mr. Dressup*. In terms of atmosphere and presentation, the two shows could hardly be less alike. Mr. Dressup pottered around his house and had unhurried conver-

Mr. Dressup, Finnegan, Casey, and the Tickle Trunk

sations with Casey and Finnegan about ordinary, everyday life. *Sesame Street* hummed with frenetic energy as numbers and letters were shouted out, sets changed every few minutes and props clanged and banged.

Had Ernie Coombs worried about the show's predicted ruin, he would have spent his time needlessly. Although *Sesame Street* was well received by Canadian children, it was *Mr. Dressup* for whom they reserved their love and reverence. There were times in the 1970s when *Mr. Dressup* had 500,000 viewers per day, with ratings often exceeding those for *Sesame Street*.

In the early years *Mr. Dressup* was taped in Studio One at the old CBC building in Toronto. Later it was moved to Studio Four, a space about the size of four classrooms that the CBC rented in a warehouse on Yonge Street. Studio Four did not have a control room so the CBC set up a mobile control unit in a truck and parked it just outside the building. When the CBC moved to its new headquarters on Front Street in

1992 it phased out Studio Four. Today the warehouse is a large retail store.

Mr. Dressup's house was a happy place, decorated in bright, primary colours, with a gold couch in front of a bay window. Near the couch stood the Tickle Trunk, and behind it toys filled a set of shelves. Mr. Dressup presided over his projects at a counter, and sometimes an easel stood ready nearby. More toys were arranged on shelves behind the counter, and on the wall hung a framed, plywood cutout of Wise Old Owl. Occasionally Mr. Dressup asked a question of Wise Old Owl, whose eyes moved when his name was called. The camera would then zoom in on Wise Old Owl while he answered, with Ernie providing his voice.

The kitchen, which consisted of a sink, counter and lower cupboards, was wheeled onto the set only when it was needed for a story. Most stories required just the couch, the main area, and the French doors that led to Mr. Dressup's yard.

The studio also included the "outdoors." Mr. Dressup's back yard was decorated with artificial greenery and bordered by a grey picket fence. Just beyond the fence stood a large tree where Casey lived with Finnegan in a tree house. Segments of almost every story included the tree house and often the camera would film Mr. Dressup going from his back door through the yard and over to Casey's house.

Because the studio was small, other sets would be placed temporarily in the space near the tree house, as they were needed. The interior set for Casey's house was one; the trading post, occasionally operated by the

An early CBC television studio

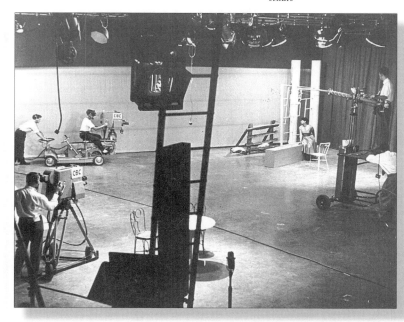

puppet, Alligator Al, was another.

By the beginning of the 1990s almost twenty people were involved in the production of *Mr. Dressup*. As well as the performers, there were three camera operators, two in the "house" and one "outside." A sound technician operated the main "boom" microphone, which hung out of sight over Mr. Dressup's head. Two set decorators arranged the props for every scene and two stagehands helped with whatever task needed doing. Two musicians provided all of the show's music, including the opening tune.

A studio director and lighting technician were also in the studio, while the producer, script assistant and as many as three technicians kept things running smoothly in the control room.

Mr Dressup with Casey and Finnegan in their tree house

While viewers at home saw a show that moved at a seemingly easy pace, the production schedule was hectic and intense. Each week four new segments were produced. The show that was broadcast on the fifth day was usually a rerun.

The shows were produced live to tape, which meant that once the cameras rolled they continued uninterrupted until the entire half-hour had been filmed. This was done for budget reasons because retakes slowed down the schedule and therefore cost more money.

Ernie's three-day work week began with a full-day script meeting, typically from 9:00 a.m. to 6:00 p.m., where the scripts for the week's segments would be reviewed and further developed. This would be followed by two days of preparation and taping in the studio. A studio day would start at 8:30 a.m. with a rehearsal of all the music and songs to be included in the segment. Over the years, guitarist Hank Monis and pianists Lois Pearson and Donald Himes (who composed the show's opening tune) all served as live musicians for the show.

Next came a rough rehearsal, followed by revisions to the script as required. Scripts were not meant to be memorized and followed word for word; rather, their purpose was to keep the show on track in terms of time and story line. Such an approach allowed for creative and spontaneous dialogue between Ernie and the puppeteers, especially in the years Judith Lawrence gave life to Casey and Finnegan. Judith allowed Casey a mind of his own and often, with the cameras rolling, he would go off on tangents not written into the script. The dialogue was so natural that Ernie sometimes forgot he was talking to a puppet.

"Did you hear what Casey said to me in rehearsal just now?" he once caught himself asking Judith Lawrence after they'd finished practising a segment.

Following the rough rehearsal, Ernie would fine-tune the day's craft, drawings or dialogue and then join the entire team for a mid-morning meeting to discuss areas still needing work. After this came a dress rehearsal and then a final meeting to iron out any remaining wrinkles. At last the show was ready to be taped without interruption.

After lunch the morning's schedule was repeated for the second segment. Rarely would Ernie leave the studio before 6:00 p.m.

The taping season started in mid-September and continued until mid-April or early May, with a short break at Christmas. At one time, 120 shows were produced during a single season, but this number was eventually reduced to a more manageable 84 and then, in the 1990s, to 79. The shows usually aired two to four weeks after they were produced.

While the pace in the studio was necessarily brisk, the atmosphere was usually calm and friendly. The *Mr. Dressup* team functioned well together and was often kept entertained by Ernie's light-hearted wit and good-natured reaction to a practical joke. One time the team was preparing for a story that required three dozen toy mice. The story was later dropped from the script but the props technician had already crafted the furry little creatures with their tiny pink ears and limp black tails. So he brought them into the studio anyway and scattered them around, hoping to make Ernie laugh during filming.

Ernie was acting out an entirely different story and ignored the mice, but they were everywhere, every time he took a step or turned around. While the crew tittered in the background, Ernie kept a straight face, manoeuvred around the furry obstacles, and continued with his script.

One mouse had been placed on the main microphone, which hung just above Ernie's head. Suddenly he reached up, grabbed it and stuffed it into his mouth with only the tail protruding. Then he calmly carried on in his Mr. Dressup role. It took several minutes before the crew could stop laughing and continue with the show.

Occasionally the studio sparkled with unintentional humour. One show opened to a scene of Ernie wielding a pipe wrench under his kitchen sink. "I had a leak in the sink," he explained as he straightened up and wiped his hands on a towel. Unaware that his statement could be misinterpreted, he continued talking about fixing the plumbing. The crew, however, caught the double meaning and instantly clapped their hands over their mouths. Judith Lawrence, who was scrunched behind the sink with Casey and Finnegan, had to work hard to stifle her own laughter. Not helped by the giggles and snickering she could hear on her headset, she had only seconds to compose herself before it was time for Casey's first line.

Although Ernie never realized his faux pas until later, he

did wonder during the filming why the crew seemed so amused. Still, the segment aired as it was played, a few weeks later.

That Ernie Coombs loved children and loved being like a child himself is without dispute. "I'm only doing what a father would do for his own children," he once replied when asked if he didn't occasionally feel

Ernie drew pictures and painted all his life

silly being Mr. Dressup. Like any good father, he addressed the children warmly, patiently, individually and honestly. He showed a genuine interest in their world. He discussed their challenges—such as learning to share and take turns—and gave them a calm and secure haven to visit for thirty minutes each weekday morning.

Small wonder the show was a hit. Altogether, nearly 4,000 episodes were produced by the CBC.

Chapter 7
Ernie Coombs, Family Man

Ernie with his children, Cathie and Chris

That Mr. Dressup aptly played the role of a caring father is not surprising, considering that Ernie Coombs was a loving and devoted father to Cathie, born in Pittsburgh in 1962, and Chris, born in Toronto in 1965. Even at the height of his fame and popularity he remained, first and foremost, a man devoted to his family.

Ernie and Lynn had a loving marriage, an equal partnership filled with trust and joy. Like Ernie's parents a generation earlier, they believed in sharing household and parenting duties. Their easy conversations with each other often had a humorous undercurrent and their approach to life was optimistic and light-hearted. Adults and children alike were welcome visitors to their home, first in Thornhill and later in the Pickering countryside.

While Ernie tried hard not to be Mr. Dressup at home, his own personality and interests were so similar that it was sometimes a challenge to keep the two identities separate. He tackled any project with enthusiasm and creative flair, and especially enjoyed making something out of materials on hand. As youngsters his children had no need for colouring books since Ernie would draw them pictures that were far more challenging and interesting.

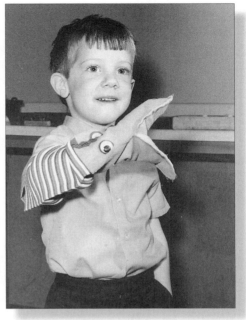

Chris Coombs age 4

Cathie Coombs age 4

As his children got older he was happy to help them with school projects, guiding and making suggestions but always resisting the temptation to take over. He often made their school lunches and would decorate the brown bags with cartoons showing some aspect of school life in a humorous way. Chris recalls that during his adolescent years his lunch bag became a coveted item that helped increase his popularity with peers, including the girls. "Everyone wanted to take it home."

Ernie's passion for working with his hands did not diminish as he grew older, even when other commitments competed for his time. When Cathie was about nine years old he built a stable and barn in the backyard for her pony. Several years later he had the house enlarged and did all of the finishing work with Lynn's help. They built the cabinets and fireplace, then laid the wood flooring, using boards Ernie rescued from an old church floor.

He also loved tinkering on old cars, trying

Ernie and his 1932 Auburn

to coax new life into spent motors and restoring the vintage bodies to their original glory. Under a car hood he happily tuned out much of his surroundings, including repeated calls to come to dinner. Although he always had a few vehicles to work on, the 1932 Auburn, his first car—long since retired from the road—remained his favourite.

Over the years the always hands-on Ernie created much of Mr. Dressup's wardrobe himself, often using coats he found at second-hand stores. In his hands the tattered cast-offs became delightfully original costumes, including a spider, a dragon, a pirate and a "bone man" decorated with various sized bones of papier mâché. Chris and Cathie had access to these costumes, a perk they capitalized on especially at Halloween.

"I was always the best-dressed kid at Halloween parties," Cathie recalls. Chris went one entrepreneurial step further—coming home with a bag filled with treats, he would change into another costume, grab an empty sack and visit the neighbourhood all over again.

A product of the Depression era, Ernie reused and recycled long before Blue Boxes began dotting the Canadian curbside. As a child he had been taught to not be wasteful, and as an adult he firmly believed that it was wrong to fill your garbage can with things that could be reused and recycled. His children often teased him for his frugality, for making a fly swatter out of a coat hanger, a piece of screen and duct tape, when $1.99 would have bought him one. His motive wasn't

Lynn and Ernie, in his spider costume, Hallowe'en 1991

rooted in poverty or stinginess; on the contrary he had always been generous with his time and money, even in the days before becoming financially well established. No, inventing a new use for materials that had outgrown their original purpose was just another enjoyable way for Ernie to be creative.

Typically, Ernie's generosity was quietly expressed and drew little attention to himself. For years the Coombs family supported a foster child in India. Closer to home, they rescued a vulnerable teenage boy and helped him stabilize his life. Ernie and Lynn met Barry Brown in the fledgling years of *Mr. Dressup* when Ernie was volunteering with Tyro, a club for teenage boys organized by St. Luke's United Church in Toronto. Every Tuesday night about two dozen boys, many from financially or socially disadvantaged families, met for crafts, games and storytelling. Ernie was a natural leader who genuinely enjoyed the company of the boys and volunteer youth leaders who helped out. Most likely none of the teens knew of his television work since their own preschool days had preceded the launch of *Butternut Square* and *Mr. Dressup*.

Barry Brown was one of the youth leaders who felt drawn to Ernie. Barry was a good-hearted high school student burdened by financial and emotional issues in his own family,

Barry Brown

including alcoholism and violence. Barry and Ernie became good friends and although Ernie never pressed for details, he soon realized that all was not well in the Brown family. One evening he said to the youth, "If you ever need to come to my house for a while, just give me a call."

Several months later Barry made the call, met Ernie at the studio, and came home with him that night. He would share the Coombs household for the next two years and become like a member of the family. Ernie and Lynn's own children were barely out of their toddler years then, but the notion of parenting a high school student didn't worry them. In Ernie's family background there had always been plenty of love to go around. Lynn's mixed memories of her own childhood enabled her to empathize with Barry and before long she began referring to him tenderly as her "son-in-love."

Barry grew to love the Coombs family and the safe and happy home they provided. Here he could relax and be completely accepted. He spent many evenings chatting with Ernie in his workshop after Cathie and Chris had been put to bed. He fell naturally into the rhythms of family life and marvelled at the energy and devotion Ernie and Lynn had for every family member, himself included. The dynamics of his own family had been so different.

Previously a mediocre student, Barry now felt motivated to do well, even to the point of signing up for student council and theatre. After graduation he left for university but, like any cherished son, would return for Christmas holidays, special occasions and family vacations in Maine. Typical of most university students, his luggage often included a bulging bag of dirty laundry.

Barry went on to a successful career in hospital administration, then later returned to school to complete a doctorate degree in gerontology, the study of aging and the elderly.

During Barry's high school years Lynn obtained a degree in early childhood education, a move prompted by her son Chris's unsatisfactory nursery school experience. Chris was an energetic and spontaneous child who had difficulty adjusting to an environment that emphasized rules, routines and enforced nap times. Lynn felt strongly that young children should be allowed some freedom for spontaneous learning, but her concerns fell on deaf ears at her son's preschool.

This experience prompted Lynn to establish the *Butternut Tree Learning Centre*, where the emphasis would be on supporting a child's creativity rather than on strict rules for behaviour. She and Ernie bought an old schoolhouse and turned it into a bright and cheerful space for preschoolers. The basement became a large tricycle room filled with ride-on toys. Not surprisingly, the centre was a big success, with enrollment eventually climbing to over 100 students. It remained in operation until the early 1990s, when Ernie and Lynn began winding down to retirement.

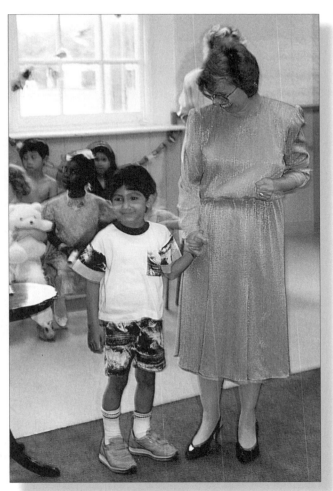

Lynn with student at the Butternut Tree Learning Centre

While the centre was Lynn's business, it served an important purpose for Ernie as well. "I would run things by her actually, and say, 'Do you think that a child this old would understand this concept?' And she would tell me."

Throughout his life Ernie Coombs maintained close ties with his family and friends in Maine. Every summer he, Lynn

Lynn, Ernie and his father, Kenneth, enjoying lobster in Maine

and the children would drive the twelve hours from Toronto back to the beloved land of his youth. Sometimes they camped along the way, Ernie taking on the job of camp leader and entertaining everyone with his diverse repertoire of comical voices and characters. Lynn would often join in with her own slapstick comedy, to the delight of the youngsters.

At their summer home in Maine, first in Pemequid Bay and later a cottage in New Harbor that remains in the family today, they roamed the bay in their boat and took picnics to the many islands scattered on the horizon. They hiked and swam and hosted summer feasts for friends and relatives. Here, as at their home in Pickering, guests were always enthusiastically received.

Ernie's old friend Bud Littlefield and his family stopped by one day with a feed of lobster. While the crustaceans were boiling in the pot Ernie went out to his shop to look for some tools to crack them open. He came back with an assortment of hammers screwdrivers and pliers. He put a pair of pliers next to a plate, then called to Lynn, "Is it pliers on the right and hammers on the left or the other way around?"

In Canada Ernie and Lynn had numerous friends, including several couples in their Pickering neighbourhood. They thrived on company and enjoyed cooking and entertaining. Their cozy dinner parties were often the setting for an evening of fun and easy camaraderie. They could have socialized with Toronto's elite, especially at the height of Ernie's career, but they preferred the company of their own friends and rarely attended gala events.

While Mr. Dressup went on to fame and acclaim, Ernie Coombs purposely did not. He loved his Mr. Dressup work and character, but never to the point where it burdened or imposed on his family life. Anyone who knew him well had no doubt of this.

Chapter 8
The Years of Change and Challenge

By the mid-1970s *Mr. Dressup* had become a household name. While this was largely due to the show's appeal, the fact that there wasn't much else on television also fuelled its success. This was the era before cable television and satellite dishes. Video games and computers, too, were still in the future. So, on any given weekday morning, chances were good that most Canadian children with access to a television set were tuned in to *Mr. Dressup*.

Inevitably the show's success germinated the idea of a Mr. Dressup road show, which Ernie's new manager, Don Jones, began organizing early in the 1980s. The style would be familiar to *Mr. Dressup* fans: there would be singing, puppets and skits featuring the kindly Mr. Dressup. Aside from Ernie, the crew would consist of an energetic musician or two who could also work the puppets. The show would play, it was correctly predicted, to an audience mostly made up of preschoolers and their parents.

The tours usually took place outside of the *Mr. Dressup* production season, but the occasional weekend

Ernie and Jim Parker with "Alex"

jaunt to a nearby city was not uncommon once demand for the show increased.

One of the musicians hired for the production was singer and guitarist Jim Parker, recruited at the last minute for an Ottawa show when the regular performer was suddenly stricken with laryngitis. Jim, who had been working with a touring version of the TV Ontario children's show, *Polka Dot Door*, hopped a train from Toronto and arrived in time to do his first show with Ernie. With little time to prepare and a great deal of anxiety, he went on stage and played several wrong notes and chords.

He expected outrage from Ernie but instead received support and encouragement. Not only had Ernie found Jim's performance funny, but, he confided, he himself also suffered the occasional anxiety attack. He knew first-hand how scary it could be to stand in front of an expectant audience and then freeze without warning. You'll work out just fine, he assured the young entertainer.

Mr. Dressup meeting a fan after a live performance

In every town the beloved Mr. Dressup was welcomed with open arms. Each child in every audience claimed him as his or her own. After all, hadn't he spoken to them personally on their living room television set all those mornings? Now he was coming for a real visit.

Ernie responded graciously to the endless clamour for autographs; the only exception was when a request came during his meal. But even then he remained friendly, inviting the autograph seeker to come back after he'd finished eating.

The demand for the show eventually took it to every part of Canada including the Far North. In some years Ernie and his team delivered more than 100 performances. Thousands of kilometres were logged on the tour bus, often late at night and

The Years of Change and Challenge **47**

Judith Lawrence

after a roadside stop for a quick meal. There was always another town waiting, another deadline to meet. At least once a blinding snowstorm forced them onto the road's shoulder where they remained stranded overnight. For several years the touring trinity consisted of the bus, the stage and the hotel.

While the pace was physically draining, the days on the road reinforced the comfortable friendship that existed among the crew. As in his younger days, Ernie loved to play practical jokes on his unsuspecting colleagues. He might hide Jim's guitar two minutes before show time or try to distract him during a skit by staring quizzically at his head as if something was stuck in his hair. Sometimes he crossed his eyes while Jim delivered his lines, and once they both started laughing so hard they had to pause to regain their composure.

One of Ernie's favourite skits was his pirate routine, which involved a balloon sword and a chair as the villain. As the "brave" pirate he skulked around the chair, pretending to be deathly afraid of it. The chair had a nail sticking out of the seat and when the pirate finally mustered up the courage to come close enough to bop it with the balloon sword, the sound of the balloon bursting sent him fleeing backstage. After he'd "recovered" from his fright he'd come back on stage only to be chased around and around by a toy lion on wheels, not "realizing" he was holding the string attached to the lion.

As with the television segments, each stage show developed a life of its own through spontaneous gags and ad-libbed lines. Both the audience and performers loved it.

Meanwhile, changes were in the air at CBC Television in Toronto. In 1991, Judith Lawrence, puppeteer for Casey and Finnegan, decided to retire and move to Hornby Island in British Columbia. While the thought of leaving saddened her, she felt the time had come to put her creative energies into other projects, such as the environment and global peace. She looked forward to leaving Toronto and wanted to experience some new adventures while she was still young enough to do so.

There was no talk of having Casey and Finnegan carry on without her; everyone knew the lively puppets were so much a part of Judith that they would have been strangers with anyone else. So they, too, moved with Judith and retired to a suitcase under her bed.

Because Mr. Dressup, Casey and Finnegan had been an interdependent trio from the days of *Butternut Square*, Judith's departure triggered considerable discussion about whether the show could successfully continue on its own. Some felt the time had come to phase out *Mr. Dressup*, while others were certain there were still some good years ahead for the show.

Ernie and Lynn skiing with their grandson Curtis

"When Casey and Finnegan left, it was a little bit like my kids growing up and leaving home," Ernie said in a later interview. "Judith had her own particular way of going through rehearsals and her own particular wit that I liked a lot."

Ernie was by now 64 years old and he and Lynn had been discussing their own retirement as well. They were grandparents and had recently celebrated their thirtieth wedding anniversary. The thought of having more time for family and golf, a game they both thoroughly enjoyed, appealed to them. And yet, they were still healthy and energetic and understandably reluctant to begin folding a career just at its peak. So in the end, Ernie chose to carry on as Mr. Dressup and the CBC continued with the show.

During Judith's last season, Casey and Finnegan began making fewer appearances, both to soften their inevitable leaving and allow for the gradual introduction of new puppets. "Chester the Crow," "Annie" and "Truffles" appeared, as well as a boy named "Alex," operated by Jim Parker. In the end the only viewers really traumatized by the change were not the children, but adults, who, after ten years of not watching *Mr. Dressup*, turned on their television sets and wondered where Casey and Finnegan had gone.

On the afternoon of May 21, 1992, Ernie was wrapping up the last segment of the show's twenty-fifth season. It had been an especially long winter, what with Judith leaving and new people in the studio, and he was looking forward to some time away from television. A staff party was scheduled for late afternoon; Lynn would be coming for the celebration and afterwards they would go out for dinner and an evening at the theatre. Likely they would discuss their children, grandchildren and vacation plans. No doubt the summer would include another trip to their beloved Maine cottage.

Lynn was coming from Pickering by train. Because the weather was so pleasant, she decided to take an earlier train, get off before her regular stop and walk the rest of the way. The stroll would be invigorating, and window-shopping on Toronto's colourful Yonge Street was always an adventure.

Suddenly, out of nowhere, a car came careening up on the sidewalk. Before Lynn could react it struck her, killing her instantly. It was later determined that the driver had suffered a seizure, causing his body to become rigid. No longer conscious and with his foot pressing down on the gas pedal, he sent the car roaring across the street and up on the sidewalk where Lynn was walking.

Barry Brown was driving to Cathie's house when a news report on his car radio disclosed that a pedestrian had been struck and killed in downtown Toronto. The woman's identity had not yet been made public. Barry knew of Lynn's plans for the afternoon and, without knowing why, felt a shiver go through his body.

At Cathie's they waited anxiously for more news. Before long a policeman, who was also a neighbour, came to the door to confirm the tragedy. Ernie, having been told at the studio and by now in deep shock, was driven home by a colleague.

Thus ended a day that had started with so much promise.

Lynn and Ernie

Chapter 9
From Mister to Doctor

Lynn's death left Ernie devastated but typically, he kept his grief private. Most likely he leaned on the people closest to him—Cathie, Chris and Barry Brown, brother Kenneth and close friend Don Jones. Other friends and colleagues offered their support and worried about him while he quietly struggled through his sorrow.

Just one month after the tragedy, Ernie was to appear on another popular children's show, *Fred Penner's Place*, an arrangement that had been scheduled much earlier in the season. Fred encouraged Ernie to postpone but Ernie, feeling that Lynn would have wanted him to carry on, insisted on keeping his commitment. A challenging moment came near the end of the show when he and Fred sang a gentle song about leaving, saying goodbye and looking forward to being together again tomorrow.

"I don't know how we were able to finish taping the show," Fred recalled. "It was a beautiful, sensitive moment, and it will always be the defining connection for me with Mr. Dressup."

In time Ernie managed to regain much of his earlier, happy personality, but talk of Lynn's death always brought a lump to his throat.

Ernie and Lynn had always planned to retire to Maine and had therefore retained their American citizenship. But in recent years, and with grandchildren now living in Ontario, they'd started thinking about staying in Pickering and becoming Canadian citizens. Ernie, especially, was ready to pledge allegiance to the country that had offered him so much opportunity and success.

Now he forged ahead alone with his application and in 1994, during the Canada Day celebration on Ottawa's Parliament Hill, he was one of 130 people to receive his citizenship. The crowd, close to 100,000 people, was peppered with signs reading, "We love you, Mr. Dressup." After the ceremony he gamely performed a patriotic rap number with the verse: "My name is Mr. Dressup, you can call me Mr. D!"

Now almost 67 years old, Ernie had been hedging against retirement for some time. "I've gotten so identified with Mr. Dressup it would be scary to wake up and just be me," he joked in a 1994 interview.

On the other hand, there was much in life he still wanted to do. He planned to take up painting again—in his youth he had produced beautiful watercolours of coastal Maine— and he wanted to restore his beloved 1932 Auburn and take it back out on the road. He looked forward to spending more time with his children and grandchildren and renewing all the old connections in Maine.

Ernie and his granddaughter Laura

And so he finally decided that the show would come to an end. On February 14, 1996, twenty-nine years and one day after *Mr. Dressup* first began, Ernie headed into the studio to tape the last segment. With emotion in his voice he thanked everyone on the production team for their help. "You made me what I am today. You know that and I appreciate it," he said, then picked up his scissors and got busy with his final project.

Because he didn't want to upset his viewers with a final goodbye, he performed as if this were just another segment, concluding with his usual, "So long, until next time." The

In his retirement Ernie decorated Bristol Area Library in Bristol, Maine, part of an addition designed by Ernie's brother and dedicated to his mother

CBC then seamlessly switched over to reruns, which continue to be aired to this day.

But Ernie Coombs didn't sit still for long. Even though the Mr. Dressup stage show he had been doing for almost fifteen years was also winding down, Don Jones was busy putting together a new tour. This one was called *Tales from the Tickle Trunk* and would take Ernie to university campuses across Canada.

"I talk about what it was like to be Mr. Dressup, how I got to be this way, funny things that happened on the road, at shows and in the studio," he told one campus newspaper reporter. "The college kids love it and I love them."

Other projects came Ernie's way, to the point where he was almost busier in retirement than he had been before. He lent his name and golfing talents to the Peter Gzowski Invitational Golf Tournaments for literacy, founded by radio broadcaster Peter Gzowski to raise funds to help people learn to read and write. These charity events took him to many provinces as well as Nunavut and the Northwest Territories.

On one occasion, Don Jones tried to special-order a pair of Velcro golf shoes for Ernie for an upcoming tournament but was told the pro shop didn't carry them. "They're for Mr. Dressup," he explained.

"Mr. Jones," the employee said from behind the counter, "Mr. Dressup taught me how to tie my shoes. He doesn't need Velcro!"

Ernie continued as spokesperson for Save the Children Canada, an organization that combats child poverty and advocates for children's rights in Canada and abroad. He volunteered his time to numerous fundraising and public awareness campaigns across the country.

Poster from Peter Pan

In 1998 he returned to live theatre with Ross Petty Productions in Toronto, cast as the Emperor of China in the play, *Aladdin*. Like other projects by Ross Petty Productions, *Aladdin* was based on the English pantomime tradition. There was plenty of room for corny jokes, cheeky humour and plot twists, exactly the sort of thing Ernie loved.

Aladdin began with the curtain rising on an empty stage. Just as the hushed audience was beginning to fidget and wonder what was wrong, a lone figure stepped out of the audience, onto the stage and walked toward the back. When he turned around, the audience went wild at the sight of Ernie Coombs.

"Oh, hello," he said, "I heard there was a show going on but I guess there's no one here ... can you help me put on a show?" Then suddenly the Tickle Trunk rose up through the stage floor. Ernie opened it and out came the costumes, the props, even the actors—everything required for the show. Lastly, a costume emerged for Ernie and as he donned it he was transformed into the Emperor right before the audience's eyes.

For the next two years he returned to Ross Petty Productions, first in 1999 to play the cash-strapped "Baron Hardup," father of Cinderella, and then as the narrator of *Peter Pan* in 2000.

In June of 2001 Ernie Coombs received an honorary doctorate degree from Trent University in Peterborough, Ontario. In his speech during the ceremony, Ernie told his fellow graduates: "Keep an open mind, and an open heart. Don't take life too seriously—it doesn't last forever, you know. And may I remind you for the last time, keep your crayons sharp, your sticky tape untangled, and always put the top back on your markers."

Chapter 10
Private Glimpses and Personal Tributes

While the private and public images of Ernie Coombs were true to each other, there was, of course, more to him than the unfailingly jovial character of stage and screen. In terms of his personal values and beliefs, he followed his heart and refused to be limited to traditional thinking. Throughout his life in both Canada and the United States, he happily shied away from organized politics, choosing instead to support social and environmental causes in a non-partisan way. According to his son Chris, he had little patience for flawed political schemes and wasted tax dollars. Instead, by word and example he taught his children the value of human life and individual rights, including the rights of women, children and culturally disadvantaged people. He had friends of every race and creed.

Ernie with his grand-daughter Caitlin

Although raised a Christian, his personal connection to a divine presence was largely rooted in the wonders of nature and the joy of everyday life. He had high moral standards but never preached about them or imposed them on others. He respected other people's choices in life and guided his own children through discussion rather than with orders.

At home Ernie preferred radio to television and relaxed with classical music while chopping vegetables and preparing dinner. A good cook, he enjoyed experimenting with new ingredients and took his time making meals from scratch. He loved hosting family dinners and often prepared four or five side dishes to accompany the main dish.

His grandchildren were dear to his heart and he supported them in all of their ventures. He once accompanied grandson Curtis to school to prove to his class that Mr. Dressup was indeed the youngster's grandfather. "Now Curtis," the disbelieving teacher had said earlier when Curtis had volunteered the information, "I'm sure everybody would love to have Mr. Dressup for their grandfather."

Ernie on a motorcycle, wearing a bucket on his head

"Grampy was pretty laid back," recalls granddaughter Caitlin. "He put a lot of effort into everything, even if it was just to have a good time."

Bud Littlefield remembers Ernie telling him how he was standing in line at a bank in Maine once when he noticed a little boy staring at him. "It finally occurred to Ernie that the boy realized he was Mr. Dressup. Ernie said he smiled at the boy and gave him a little wave. The boy's face lit up with a huge smile. Ernie said to me, 'I felt like Santa Claus.' He didn't say, 'I felt like a big star.' He felt like Santa Claus. That was typical Ernie."

"Ernie was always so easy to work with in the studio and at our script meetings," says Susan Sheehan, Mr. Dressup producer from 1989 to 1996. "He never lost his temper, never yelled or said mean things. He was such a gentleman with never any flashes of "star" temperament. However, when he felt he was right about something, he could really dig in his heels."

"He was just the most humble of men," remembers Ross Petty of Ross Petty Productions. "He had no concept of his fame. He was really a man of the people, just happy to greet people with no signs of show if they came up to him, which many did. He was just happy to be part of humanity."

Chapter 11
Laid to Rest

Ernie Coombs died on September 18, 2001, from complications of a stroke suffered eight days earlier. He was seventy-three years old. While the family kept details of his passing private, the nation began mourning his sudden and untimely death. Coming as it did on the heels of the September 11 terrorist attack on America, many people couldn't help but think the world was unravelling at its seams.

To ease the finality of the loss of Ernie Coombs and Mr. Dressup, CBC Television organized a tribute and invited everyone to their Toronto studio for the afternoon. Chris Coombs welcomed the audience wearing his father's favourite spider costume. Judith Lawrence brought Casey and Finnegan from British Columbia for one last appearance. "Mr. Dressup's not here anymore and we're pretty sad about that," Casey said in his usual straightforward way.

Fred Penner sang about being together again tomorrow and Don Jones talked about the adventures he and Ernie had shared while on tour. The Tickle Trunk stood in the middle of the stage. Everyone laughed a little and cried a little.

On July 20, 2002, Ernie Coombs's ashes were laid to rest in Chamberlain Cemetery in Round Pond, Maine, next to his parents and wife, Lynn. The family gathered under a clear blue sky. Five of his high school friends, Charles Hatch included, came and brought flowers. There were cousins, friends and neighbours, "a great family group with no pretense, that was glad to be together and use the occasion, sad as it was, to connect with each other," Charles Hatch remembers.

The minister had at one time lived near the Coombs family in Round Pond and knew them well. He spoke of Ernie as a friend and neighbour. Chris Coombs also said a few words in tribute, this time wearing Ernie's pirate vest, the one festooned all over with zippers that have nothing to zip.

Ernie on the golf course

"When one gets to a certain age and they are talking to their children," he said, "they stop, catch themselves and say, 'Oh God, I'm becoming my father.' I stop, catch myself and say, 'Thank God I'm becoming my father.'"

In memory of Ernie Coombs and to continue his charitable work, the Coombs family organized the Annual Ernie Coombs Memorial Golf Tournament. Each year participants play for the Marlene Coombs Cup, named in honour of Ernie's beloved wife, Lynn. All proceeds go to Save The Children Canada.

The first tournament, which raised almost $18,000, was held in Toronto on September 17, 2002. Ernie's 1932 Auburn, finally restored just a few years before his death, was proudly on display. Had Ernie been there he would have smiled and been quietly pleased. He might have told a little joke or two. Then he would have gathered up his clubs and invited everyone to come join him on the fairway.

Ernie Coombs

1927	Ernest Arthur Coombs is born in Auburn, Maine, on November 26
1928	Moves to Waterville, Maine
1942	Moves to Yarmouth, Maine and enrolls in North Yarmouth Academy
1945	Graduates from high school and signs up for two years military service as a weatherman in the Philippines
1947	Enrolls in a two-year program at the Vesper George School of Art in Boston
1952	Works on television pilot for owners of Boothbay Playhouse
	Marries his first wife, Margo, an actor with the Boothbay Playhouse
1954	Separates from Margo
1959	Moves to Pittsburgh and meets Marlene "Lynn" Hodgkiss
	Becomes a puppeteer for *Dimple Depot* on WQED TV in Pittsburgh
1961	Marries Lynn Hodgkiss
1962	Daughter Cathie is born in Pittsburgh; Ernie moves his family to Toronto, Canada, and joins the *Mr. Rogers* team on CBC Television
1964	Stars in *Butternut Square* on CBC Television and creates Mr. Dressup character
1965	Son Chris is born
1967	CBC cancels *Butternut Square* and creates *Mr. Dressup* to replace it
c 1982	*Mr. Dressup* goes on the road as a stage show
1991	Judith Lawrence retires, along with Casey and Finnegan
1992	Lynn is hit by a car and killed
1994	Ernie becomes a Canadian citizen
	Receives Earle Grey Award for excellence in Canadian television
1996	Tapes last *Mr. Dressup* show on February 14, Receives Gemini Award, "Children's Award" from the Children's Broadcast Institute, and the Order of Canada
2001	Receives an honorary doctorate degree from Trent University in Peterborough, Ontario
	Dies on September 18, eight days after suffering a stroke

Further Reading

Bleakney, Peter. "TV Icon Loves Old Wheels," *Toronto Star*, February 14, 1998. p. G22.

Coombs, Ernie and Shelley Tanaka. *Mr. Dressup's Book of Things to Make and Do.* Toronto: Stoddart Kids, 1991.

Gilmor, Don. "When You've Played Dress-up This Long, They Call You Mister." *Saturday Night*, April, 1994, Vol. 109 #3, p. 25.

Nash, Knowlton. *Cue the Elephant! Backstage Tales at the CBC.* Toronto: McClelland & Stewart, 1996.

Poulin, Valerie. "The Remarkable Mr. Dressup" in *Performing Arts and Entertainment in Canada.* Vol 33 #3, Autumn 2001, p. 35.

Rawlinson, H. Graham and J.L. Granatstein. *The Canadian 100: The 100 most influential Canadians of the 20th century.* Toronto: Little, Brown Canada, 1997.

Credits

The publisher wishes to thank the following for their generous assistance:

Barrie Brown, pages 37, 42
Boothbay Region Historical Society, page 17
Canadian Broadcasting Corporation, Still Photo Collection, pages 27, 30, 32, 34
Chris Coombs, pages 4, 20, 24, 51, 63
Cathie MacKinnon, pages 16, 25, 26, 38, 39, 40, 41, 43, 45, 49, 53, 57, 58, 61
Jim Parker, pages 46, 47
Judith Lawrence, page 48
Kenneth and Geraldine Coombs, pages 3, 5, 6, 7, 8, 9, 10, 11, 14, 15, 44, 54
North Yarmouth Academy Archives, Don & Marge Foster Richardson Collection, pages 12, 13
Ross Petty Productions, page 55
Toronto Telegram, page 33
Walter Littlefield, pages 18, 22, 28

Every effort has been made to credit all sources correctly. The publishers will welcome any information that will allow them to correct any errors or omissions.

Index